RUBANK BOOK OF TRUMPET SOLOS
EASY LEVEL

MEDIA INCLUDED
Recordings
Audio Accompaniments

PLAYBACK+
Speed • Pitch • Balance • Loop

T0069382

CONTENTS

Albatross..Vander Cook 3

Allerseelen Op. 10, No. 8...................................Richard Strauss/trans. Harold L. Walters 4

The Dancer..R. M. Endresen 5

Falcon..Vander Cook 6

Kinglet..Vander Cook 7

Legend..V. Shelukov/ed. Wm. Gower 8

Meadowlark..Vander Cook 9

Oriole..Vander Cook 10

Scherzo..V. Shelukov/ed. Wm. Gower 11

Starling..Vander Cook 12

The Victor..R. M. Endresen 13

Waltz Chromatic..R. M. Endresen 14

Warbler..Vander Cook 15

To access recordings and PDF accompaniments visit:
www.halleonard.com/mylibrary

7745-5824-4988-1815

ISBN 978-1-4950-6506-4

HAL•LEONARD® CORPORATION
7777 W. BLUEMOUND RD. P.O. BOX 13819 MILWAUKEE, WI 53213

Visit Hal Leonard Online at
www.halleonard.com

Albatross

Trumpet

Vander Cook

Allerseelen

Op. 10, No. 8

Richard Strauss
Transcribed by Harold L. Walters

Trumpet

4

The Dancer

Trumpet

R.M. Endresen

Moderato tempo

Falcon

Trumpet

Vander Cook

Kinglet

Trumpet

Vander Cook

Legend

Trumpet

V. Shelukov
Edited by Wm. Gower

Meadowlark

Trumpet

Vander Cook

Oriole

Trumpet

Vander Cook

Scherzo

Trumpet

V. Shelukov
Edited by Wm. Gower

Starling

Trumpet

Vander Cook

The Victor

Trumpet

R.M. Endresen

Waltz Chromatic

Trumpet

R.M. Endresen

Warbler

Trumpet

Vander Cook